Matias Faldbakken
SEARCH / SUCHE

dOCUMENTA (13)

HATJE
CANTZ

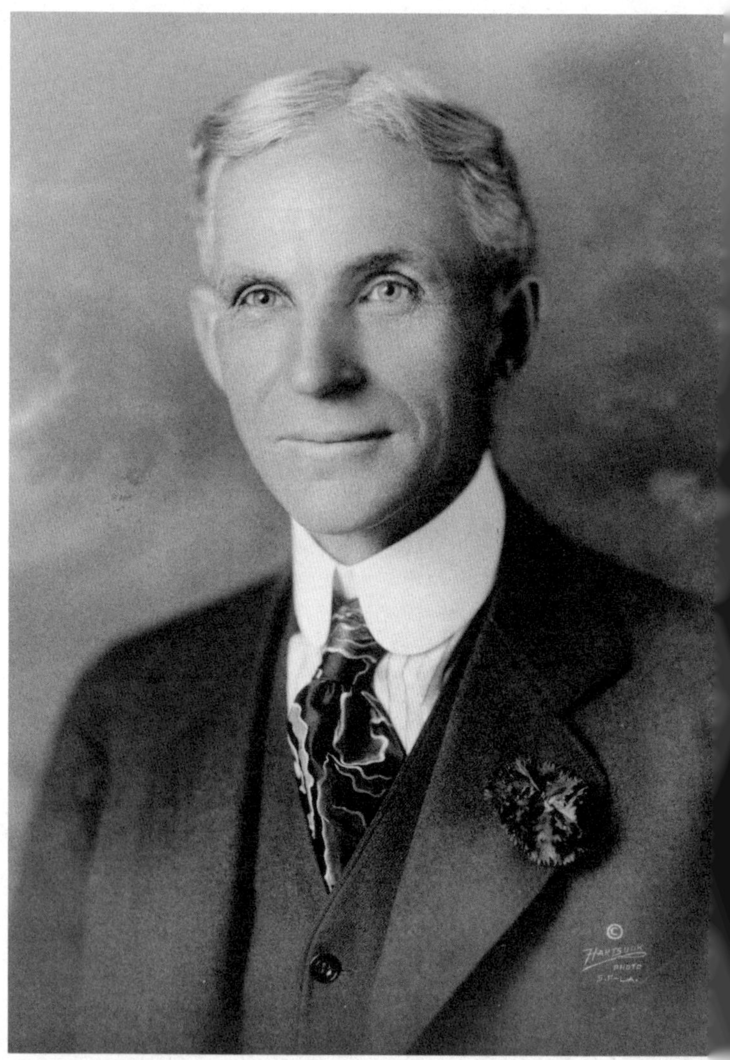

Matias Faldbakken
SEARCH / SUCHE

Henry Ford, 1919

Battle of Aachen

Spa
Aachen History Spa
Aachen History of Prostitution
Aachen Syphilis Capital

Spa Aachen
Nude Village
Nudeville
Crazy Nude Germans

Jimmy T. Kindt
Aachen Techno Kindt
Motörhead
Lemmyisms

Stone Dead Forever Lyrics

Happy Vandal
Extinguisher Vandal
Vandal Freedom
Fire Stopper

Vendôme Communard Posers
Communard Poseurs
Vendôme Erection

Pizza

TTACO
Johnny Taco

Control Yourself
Please Control Yourself

Control

Over Control
Above Control

Sponge Bob Teeth
Sponge Bob Anatomy

Frost

Franzen Asshole
Franzen Jerk

Cunt in Sloveninan
An Empty Head Gets The Easiest Sleep

Testino
Testino CANDICE
Testino Jew
TESTINO BUSINESS OF BEING ANNA

Hadrian
Hadrian Face
Aureus Of Emperor Hadrian
Greek Crunch
Parking Für Juden
National Bank of Greece Burn Me

Burn Me
Leonidas from Sparta

Overreaction
Overreaction As Content
Xeroin

Damnato Memoriae
Gerard Depardieu Wife Beater
Gerard Depardieu Butcher
Die Zeit Depardieu

Fresh

Die Paris
Awful Paris
Corrupt Paris

Schäfer
Schäfer Trash Bin
Chrome On White
Schopenhauer Misogynist

Red Banana

Complete ZZ Top Lyrics
Noble Trucker
BlackBerry
BlackBerry Brigade
BlackBerry Torch

Halloween Nose Man
Nose Person Halloween
Mr Nose Halloween
Herr Nasen

Mummy Funny
Mummyfied

Yoda Face Ppaint
Yoda Face Paint

Yoda Trompe l'Oeil

Mid Size Spoons
Theatercafeen Historical View
TC

TC Expelled
Drunk Parking
Drunk Driver Excellence
Solli BOWLING

★

Bald Again
Bald Again Lyrics

Bald To Be Wild

Snorto
Paganini

Serralves Hat Model
Christmas In Porto
Imperial Porto
Merry Christmas In Portugese
Huckleberry Finn Hat

37 cm to Inches

War and Peace (and War)

Small Violin
Child Prodigy Violin

Edgar's Lamps
"All Weather Is Passing"

Olav H Hauge Damnato Memoriae
Muskelsvinn
Kjetil Rolness Muskelsvinn

Schengen Ost

"Spill Om Livet"
P.O.R.

Jacques Prévert
Jacques Pervert

★

AUDI
AUDI A4
A4
AUDI
AUDI FLAW
AUDI HATE
AUDI DISASTER

AUDI CAR CRASH

Sebs Hotel Babes

Depressing Gourmet
Amazingly Depressing

Moonshine
Moonshine Hedemark
Jugs
Plastic Jugs
Moonshine Jugs

"Mash"
Moonshine Mash
Moonshine Jugs
Plastic Jugs

Jygs Kiquor
Lugs Liquor
Jugs Liquor

Skåne Probverbs

Rolf Wesenlund Quotes
T-Ford Race
Ford
Henry Ford Eyes
Henry Ford Eye Color
Henry Ford Color Photo
Hkenry Ford Taylor

Mittelrhein

"Pannelugg"
Fringe

Smells Like <<<<team <<spirit
Smells Like Team Spirit

★

Dry Cement Maxbo
Jerry Can Biltema

Oslo Police Christnas Party

Old Jerry Can
Jerry Can

Wehrmachtskanister
Paul Pleiss

Integrity
Septic Death Karaoke 7
Voice Of Thousands Compilation

"He Is Left-Handed And Walks With A Cane"

Goggles
Newspaper Vending Machines Cheap
Comedy Store

18 cm to Inches

The M
Melovins Lyorics
Melvins Lyrics Complete
Melvins Silver lake
Spaceland
Heisenberg

Uncertainty Principle Heisenberg

Black Stooges Lyrics
Hammer Address
MC Hammer Address

Day Of The Living Dead Screenplay
Vertigo Screenplay
Falling Down Screenplay
Breaking Bad Season 2 Screenplay
Jessie Pinkman
Pinkman House

Lash Out Lyrics
The Hills DiVello
Adam DiVello Interview
The Hills Transcript

Join, or Die
Join, or Die Ben Franklin

Rachel Whiteread
Rachel Whiteread Family
Rachel Whiteread Daughter
"Half-Brained, Half-Assed, Half-Hearted"

Hedemark Moonshiners
Myrmoen Moonshine

Griff Ass Tattoo

Dan Colen Cartoon
AvdH
AvdH Balding
First, The Good News

Santa Monica Beach Toxic
Venice Beach Toxic

Santa Monica Airlines
Santa Monica Air Centre
Natas Kaupas Porn
When Platitudes Become Form

Midway Car Rental
Midway Dodge
Barbie, I want You Back
Jack Goldstein Lightning
Jack Goldstein Metal
Jack Goof

The Day The Animals Died

Joshua Tree Casino
Palm Springs Casino
Kirk Douglas Way Palm Springs
Windmill Wings
Windmill Transport
Windmill Wing Transport

The Pigs The Pigs
Animal Depression
The Alcohol The Alcohol

Europ

EUROP

Faster And More Furious
"His Resignation Was His Confession"

The Wiener Cafe
The Wiener Cafe Madness
Bernhard Madness
Bernhard Riot
Bernhard Cafe Korb
Wiener Aktionismus Wiener Cafe
Showdown Cafe Korb

Lee Strassberg Close Up
Lee Assberg

★

Rambo
Rambo Cover
All Rambo Covers

Chubby Chaser T-Shirt

Panasonic Box
Samsung Box
Loewe Box
LED Box

The War
Title The War

There Might Be Blood

Baldor
Baldor Food
Baldorium Food
Baldorama

The Floor Shiny
Shining Floor

LED Box
LED
L.E.D.

LED Zeppelin TV
Not Hanks

Klein
SO KLEIN
SJOP KLEIN
SHOP KLEIN

Raise Plow
Raise Plow Sign
The Sun Shone, Having No Alternative, On The Nothing New

Pluck You Chicken

OFF! In Memoriam

El Paso Deaths
El Paso Murder Stats
El Paso Homicide Drugs
El Paso War
El Paso Times Obituaries

War in El Paso

700 Waco St

Marfa Train
Freight Train Through Marfa
WhataBurger Menu
Judd Arrowheads

"Whatever was mortal in Albrecht Dürer is covered by this stone"

Margaret Mead
Don't Pet A Burning Dog

Tin Tiles
Typical Revolutionist
Madero
Madero Images

Natures Bounty Melatonin 5mg
Stiga Snow Racer

Eh
Ehh
Ehhh

E.H.H.H.

Beer Chicken Recepy
Oil?

Shoe Box Monolith
Safe Monolith

Safe Tower
Safe Rod

Swastika Windmill
Tax Man
The Tax Man

Shock And Awesome

★

Icicle
Icicle Rain
Icicle Injury Oslo

LSD Berlin
YOT
Nordby Shopping
Ugh, Said The Critics

Helen Marten Drag And Drop

Abbatoirs Allee Charles De Fitte

SCRIP TITLE Written By Name of First Writer Based On, If Any

Stick Of Jerry Cans
Rod Of Jerry Cans
Jerry Can Cluster
Jerry Can Raft

Harry S Morgan
Hard Rakel Cafe

Kristinehamn History
Kristinehamn
WeiWei BlackJack

Othello Hotel

Abstract Talk

★

Nedre Rommen
APT
APT Scam
APT Pyramid

"Down Nigger Paved Streets"
William A Thigpen, Jr.

Everted Jerry Can

Vandals Vans Logo
Vandals
Poser Poseur
PPoosseeuurr

DDOOUUBBLLEE

Weber B20
OSK
"Oslo Skytter Klubb"
Joseph Beuys and the German Past, Tentatively
Radio Televizija Slovenija
Meta
Metaklikk

Deep Framing

Sausage With Sausage
Pork On Pork
Sausage with Sausage Appendix

Sierra Leone Romance

"I Want To Be A Kamakazi When I Grow Up"

Watch Without Arms

Bristol Molotow
Roddy Lumsden Bristol

N˚ARKO

Les 0 Journées de Sodome

*

F. Scott Fitzgerald The Last Coon

Honk The Horn
Hank The Horn
Horny Hank

Garage X Ensemble
Ali M. Abdullah X

Judengasse History

Batanga
Batanga Knife
Batanga Phone

Mel Ramos Photo Rong
Mel Ramos Photo Ring

Yaba
Crazy Medicine
Yaba Crazy Medicine
Yaba Traffic Mekong

Sleepy Phiyer

Zerreissprobe

Uri Geller Junkie Bend Spoon
Outline
Closet Outline
Jug Outline
Poster Outline

Ship Of Drunks
"Danskebåten"
"Danskebåten Menu"
Alcohol Ship

Alco Ship

Tarkovsky Poster Newsprint
Poster Newsprint
Gun Shells
Gun Shell Ocean
Artillery Shell Forest

HAMYSVEIS

Gun Shell Floor
Brass Floor

★

ELLE Depression
ELLE

The Readymades
Holten Art
Dragicevic Bluff

Motril Hospital
When A Jorney Begins Badly It Rarely Ends Well

★

Cowboys Stadium Price

Brass Man
The Brass Man Dallas
Gene Jones Art
Jerry Jones Net Worth
Jerry Jones Fistpumping
"Jerry Jones Just Did A Fist Pump"

Onyx price
AR-15
AR-15 Ammo
AR-15 Rapid Fire

Shutters
Shutters on the Beach

Oslo Bopmb

Oslo Bomb
Blond Terror Oslo

Oslo Blond Jihad

Utøya
Utøya Shooting

2083
Breivik 2083
Berwick 2083
2083 Utøya
Utøya Footage
Utøya Gasoline
Utøya Boat Footage
Fjordman Gates of Vienna
Fjordman Real Name
Utøya Live
Utøya Swim
Utøya Helicopter
Utøya Geography
Utøya Youth

Glock Utøya

Saga
Saga Lyrics
WoW Theme
WoW Motivationa
The Battle Of Badr

Eurabia Breivik
Will Durant India
Fertilizer Breivik
Gasoline Breivik
Glenn Beck Breivik

Cultural Suicide

★

1389 Blog
Brothers Judd

Foggy

"I Worship Not That Which You Worship"

"What To Do After The Massacre"

You Poor And Stupid
I Could Scream
Big Pharaoh
TigerHawk

JammedGun

★

Terrence Mallick
The Tree Of Life
Tree Of Life Worst Movie

Hate Terrence Mallick
Somewhere
Welding machine

PolBlog

Jerry Cans Stacked
Jerry Can Star

Mesh Container
Hassan Al-Banna
Zakat

Hamar Cathedral
Bowling
Translate Jade

XXL Golf Bag
XXL Glof Clubs
XXL Golf Clubs

Golf Bag Rocket Launcher

Golf Bag Torture

Harry Potter Scar
Dora
Bots
Boost
Boots
Hogvprt
Hogwart

Sculpoture of Fools
Sculpture of Fools
Collective Stupidity
Collective Fuckup

Lars Hedegaard

Gallia Watch

CDWRME

★

Einarsson Mask
Jerry Lewis Gas Chamber

Bård Hoksrud Taped
Bård Hoksrud The Fat Man

Baltic
Baltic Face
NGO BINGO

The Tree of Life
The Tree of Life Sucks

Terrence Mallick I Hate Hou

Terrence Mallick I Hate You

Oslo, Texas
Oslo Wenders

DowneastBlog

★

The Pigs The Pigs
"All Children, Except One, Grow Up"

Matias Faldbakken (b. 1973) lives and works as an artist and writer in Oslo.
Matias Faldbakken (geb. 1973) lebt und arbeitet als Künstler und Autor in Oslo.

Matias Faldbakken's
SEARCH

Culture is a great transcoder from text into image . . . a black box that has text for input and images for output.

—Vilém Flusser

For *SEARCH*, Matias Faldbakken went into the log of his different hard drives and extracted parts of his Google search histories. The search phrases are printed chronologically according to when they were typed into the search box.

It is a straightforward concept with a revealing and a semi-absurd end product. The texts are to a large part based on image searches. In many respects they show the verbal foundation for the artist's image production: they are partly his notes, partly his research.

These search-word texts are at the same time almost like automatic writing; unconscious (or accidental) text production. They allow the reader to witness part of his working process and could be seen as a cross section of his thinking. The texts occupy a space in between the artist's visual and textual production, ending up here as a form of (concrete) poetry.

—The Editors

Matias Faldbakkens
SUCHE

*Die Kultur ist ein großer Transcoder von Text zu Bild […] eine Black
Box, deren Input aus Text und deren Output aus Bildern besteht.*

– Vilém Flusser

Für *SEARCH* verwendete Matias Faldbakken die Protokolle
seiner verschiedenen Festplatten und extrahierte einen Teil der
Verläufe seiner Google-Recherchen. Die Suchanfragen sind
chronologisch nach den Daten abgedruckt, an denen sie in das
Suchfeld eingegeben wurden.

Dies ist ein gradliniges Konzept mit einem ebenso aufschlussrei-
chen wie einigermaßen absurden Ergebnis. Die Texte beruhen
überwiegend auf Bildrecherchen. Sie zeigen in vielerlei Hinsicht
die sprachlichen Grundlagen der Bildproduktion des Künstlers:
Sie sind teils Notizen, teils Recherche.

Gleichzeitig ähneln die Suchbegriff-Texte der *Écriture automa-
tique,* einer unbewussten (oder zufälligen) Textproduktion. Sie
ermöglichen dem Leser, einen Teil seines Arbeitsprozesses mit-
zuerleben und können als ein Querschnitt seines Denkens gelten.
Die Texte stehen zwischen der Bild- und der Textproduktion des
Künstlers und erscheinen hier als eine Art (konkreter) Poesie.

– Die Herausgeber

100 Notes – 100 Thoughts / 100 Notizen – 100 Gedanken

№035: Matias Faldbakken
SEARCH / SUCHE

dOCUMENTA (13), 9/6/2012 – 16/9/2012
Artistic Director / Künstlerische Leiterin: Carolyn Christov-Bakargiev
Member of Core Agent Group, Head of Department /
Mitglied der Agenten-Kerngruppe, Leiterin der Abteilung: Chus Martínez
Head of Publications / Leiterin der Publikationsabteilung: Bettina Funcke

Managing Editor / Redaktion und Lektorat: Katrin Sauerländer
Editorial Assistant / Redaktionsassistentin: Cordelia Marten
English Proofreading / Englisches Korrektorat: Sam Frank
Translation / Übersetzung: Barbara Hess
Graphic Design and Typesetting / Grafische Gestaltung und Satz: Leftloft
Typeface / Schrift: Glypha, Plantin
Production / Verlagsherstellung: Christine Emter
Reproductions / Reproduktionen: weyhing digital, Ostfildern
Paper / Papier: Pop'Set, 240 g/m², Munken Print Cream 15, 90 g/m²
Manufacturing / Gesamtherstellung: Dr. Cantz'sche Druckerei, Ostfildern

Illustrations / Abbildungen: p. / S. 1: documenta III, 1964, installation view with /
Installationsansicht mit Wilhelm Loth, *Signal anthropomorph*, 1960/61, and /
und Alicia Penalba, *Grande Ailée*, 1960–63 (detail / Detail), photo /
Foto: © Lederer/documenta Archiv; © Wilhelm-Loth-Stiftung, Karlsruhe;
p. / S. 2: © Library of Congress, Washington, D.C., photo / Foto: Hartsook

**documenta und Museum Fridericianum
Veranstaltungs-GmbH**
Friedrichsplatz 18, 34117 Kassel | Germany / Deutschland
Tel. +49 561 70727-0 | Fax +49 561 70727-39
www.documenta.de
Chief Executive Officer / Geschäftsführer: Bernd Leifeld

**Published by / Erschienen im
Hatje Cantz Verlag**
Zeppelinstrasse 32, 73760 Ostfildern | Germany / Deutschland
Tel. +49 711 4405-200 | Fax +49 711 4405-220
www.hatjecantz.com

ISBN 978-3-7757-2884-3 (Print)
ISBN 978-3-7757-3064-8 (E-Book)

Printed in Germany

With support by /
Mit Unterstützung von

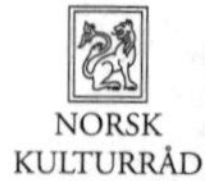
NORSK
KULTURRÅD

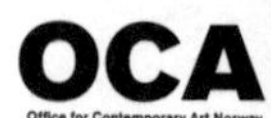

Gefördert durch die

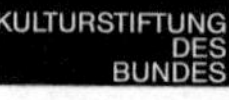

funded by the German Federal
Cultural Foundation